HOW TO USE
This Toolkit

If you can recognize a well-designed garden but need some basic skills to start building your own garden beds in interesting and beautiful ways, here's the tool you need to get started. Read up on the fundamentals of good garden design (it's not as hard as you might think), learn a simple method for creating your own design, and browse a selection of 78 reliable plants that you can find in almost any good garden center in a temperate climate. Sure, you might find newer varieties out there, but these are the classics. There are a few shrubs, lots of perennials, and a handful of plants that won't be hardy in most gardens but are worth the effort to bring indoors each winter or worth the money to buy new each spring.

Once you've studied the basics of combining plants and browsed through the possibilities, use the stickers and the fold-out design board to create the garden(s) of your dreams. We've included different cultivars for a number of plants and multiples of many of the stickers, because sometimes you need more than one. The design board has a grid on one side and an empty garden plot on the other, to suit your working style. The stickers are proportional to each other, based on final growth habit, but do keep in mind that plants grow! You'll need to take that into account when you actually start digging.

Playing with Plants

I started gardening when I was 12 years old, deadheading petunias and transplanting herb seedlings in a neighbor's greenhouse. I can still vividly recall the stickiness of the petunias on my fingers, the scent of basil seedlings as I teased their roots apart, the sight of sunbeams streaking through the potting soil dust in the air, and the sound of classical music playing on the little radio on the shelf by the wooden labels. It was a compelling experience, to say the least. I rediscovered gardening in college in an introductory horticulture class and promptly switched from doggedly pursuing a math degree to having a blast earning a horticulture degree.

After stints as an intern at an organic herb farm on Nantucket Island in Massachusetts and managing a busy nursery yard and greenhouse in Westchester County, New York, I landed at a lovely public garden in the Hudson Valley of New York, where I got a crash course in garden design. I was immersed every day in stunning examples of great gardening. Plants were used as building blocks to create incredible combinations, and by extension, whole gardens. I couldn't help but start to see how foliage and flowers interacted with each other, and what magic could be created with just a few plants and some loving care.

This exposure prepared me for my time at *Fine Gardening* magazine, where, as an editor and photographer, I traveled the country for 15 years, meeting wonderful gardeners, exploring spectacular gardens, and collecting information to share with our avid readers in new and interesting ways. I've visually dissected hundreds of stunning beds and borders that have one thing in common — they use plants in inventive and ingenious ways. Beautiful gardens may seem effortless, but behind every compelling and beautiful planting is a talented and inspired gardener who has painstakingly arranged and rearranged plants until they came together into a perfect whole.

Being exposed to gorgeous gardens is wonderful, but back in my own garden, it was hard to recreate the wonderfully lush and colorful beds I admired. I often found myself leafing through plant catalogs and garden magazines, tempted to cut out pictures of individual plants so that I could rearrange them at will. A couple of attempts made me realize how futile the exercise was. The plants were never sized accurately in relation to each other, and rarely could I find a complete and unobstructed picture of an entire plant. There was only one option: create the pictures for myself!

This toolkit is an attempt to pass on a bit of the knowledge gained from two decades of being immersed in great gardens, with stickers, a design board, and an accompanying guidebook for putting it into practice. You'll find more in-depth tomes on how to design a garden, to be sure, and even completely different techniques. But this is a good place to start, before you spend money at the nursery or expend sweat in the garden. So have fun mixing, matching, and playing with plants, dreaming of the gorgeous gardens you'll create!

— Michelle

The Keys to a Beautiful Garden

One of the most intimidating parts of gardening is deciding what plant to put where. It's easy to recognize a beautiful garden or well-designed planting. Explaining why it's beautiful is harder. And creating your own pleasing planting is even more challenging. How many times have you brought home a bunch of wonderful plants from the local nursery, arranged them in a way you thought would be attractive, planted and nurtured them, and then a few months later realized that they didn't work well together and all needed to be moved?

While gardening is all about trial and error, it can be awfully time- and energy-consuming. But the art of combining plants really comes down to practice and a few basic principles, broken down into small chunks.

Harmony + Contrast

Designing a pleasing garden planting is basically a matter of mixing and matching plants to create harmony and contrast.

Harmony is all about similarities. It makes you feel relaxed, like everything is right with the world. You can create harmony in a bed or border by combining plants with similar traits. A duo of softly mounding plants is restful and relaxing. A collection of plants with similar flower colors is soothing as well.

But too much harmony can be boring: in Example 1, the combo of fuzzy, silver-leafed 'Big Ears' lamb's ears, 'Berggarten' sage, and 'Silver Mound' wormwood — three plants with similar textures, colors, and forms — is too homogeneous. Without some sort of exciting contrast, it falls flat.

Contrast is all about differences. It creates excitement, as if you were having a heated but amicable debate with a friend. You can create contrast in a planting by combining plants with significantly different characteristics. A strongly vertical plant mixed with one that's soft and mounding highlights their differences and inspires you to look a little closer. A dark-leafed plant combined with a bright and cheery one does this as well.

But too much contrast can be jarring: in Example 2, the mix of chartreuse, blue-flowered 'Sweet Kate' spiderwort, fuzzy, silver-leafed 'Big Ears' lamb's ears, and deep, dark 'Obsidian' heuchera has too much going on. Three wildly different foliage colors, with a fourth color added to the mix from the spiderwort's flowers, plus three different leaf shapes — it's too chaotic; it needs a unifying element to create harmony.

Example 1: All three of these plants have silvery leaves and a mounding shape. The combo needs some contrast to liven it up.

Example 2: With three very different foliage colors and leaf shapes, this combo could use some harmony to pull it together.

A good mix of harmony and contrast strikes a balance between soothing similarities and exciting differences. The plants have enough in common that they naturally mix, but they offer enough differences that they don't get lost in each other or come across as boring.

In a more pleasing combo, Example 3, the aptly named purple fountain grass and the mounding silver 'Big Ears' lamb's ears create exciting color contrast, while the deep burgundy 'Obsidian' heuchera makes a harmonious color link with the purple fountain grass even as the flowers of the 'White Swan' coneflower create a color link with the lamb's ears. All four plants have differing textures and forms, but thanks to the color matches, the planting is a perfect mix of harmony and contrast!

Think of it this way: finding the perfect blend of contrast and harmony for a planting is like planning a fabulous party. You invite a bunch of friends over (buy a bunch of plants you love), making sure you have many different but pleasant personalities (include lots of beautiful colors, forms, and textures), and then selectively introduce them to each other based on their similarities and differences — just enough of each so that they can have a lively discussion without getting bored (look too similar) or getting into a fistfight (clash horribly).

As the party rolls along (the season progresses), your guests (awesome plants that they are) mingle (weave into each other), ebb (go in and out of flower), and flow (spread and interact with other plants) until everyone gets sleepy (those plants are *spent*!) and the party naturally winds down (fall sets in) and your friends (plants) say their happy goodbyes and go home (go blessedly dormant for the winter). You're ready for a rest, too, but you can't wait to do it all over again!

There are so many ways to create a pleasing mix of harmony and contrast in a planting. Let's break it down into the three main traits you should consider when choosing a plant — color, texture, and form.

Example 3: This combo shows a pleasing mix of harmony and contrast.

Color

Color is what it's all about, isn't it? Who isn't thrilled by a deep red rose, a glistening white lily, a luscious pink peony, or a sunny yellow bearded iris? But when it comes to color, think beyond flowers to foliage colors, too. While colorful flowers are crowd-pleasers, a garden can't be based on flowers alone. Flowers should be the icing on the cake that is your garden. Cake without icing is still great (though it would be even better with icing), but icing on its own is only momentarily thrilling and satisfying. With that sugar high comes a sugar crash.

So, too, with colorful flowers. Most perennials bloom only for two to three weeks, and unless you've planned very carefully and planted perennials that will bloom one after the other, and popped in a few annuals that bloom continually, there will be gaps throughout the season when nothing significant in your planting is blooming. If you haven't backed up those blooms with a tapestry of interesting foliage colors, you'll be left with a boring sea of green.

Happily, most garden centers stock a rainbow of foliage colors. Picture deep burgundy 'Royal Purple' smokebush, bright yellow and silvery blue hostas ('Sun Power' and 'Halcyon'), dusky purple 'Obsidian' heuchera, sultry black mondo grass, silvery 'Big Ears' lamb's ears, and even green plants with colorful variegation, like cream-variegated 'Color Guard' yucca.

Don't disregard green altogether, though. Consider all the shades of green, from the deep forest green of European wild ginger to the medium green of a Christmas fern to the bright, energizing chartreuse of a 'Citronelle' heuchera. Using a variety of foliage colors creates a fascinating season-long quilt of a garden upon which flowers will shine as long as they last.

Colorful flowers are thrilling but fleeting. Use them as accents instead of the main bulk of your garden.

There are so many exciting foliage colors to be found at the nursery. Burgundy, blue, silver, and yellow can stand in for colorful flowers in a garden, working hard all season rather than for just a few weeks.

'Royal Purple' smokebush

'Sun Power' hosta

'Halcyon' hosta

'Obsidian' heuchera

Black mondo grass

'Big Ears' lamb's ears

'Color Guard' yucca

Green doesn't have to be boring. There are so many different shades to choose from!

European wild ginger

Christmas fern

'Citronelle' heuchera

Flowers do, however, offer an opportunity to make your garden an ever-changing tableau. While your tapestry of foliage (and a few select plants that flower all season long) is holding down the fort, looking pretty, you can play with color by adding plants that don't garner much attention when they're not flowering but make a brief, happy splash when they are. A white-flowering plant will bring attention to a white-variegated plant (harmony). Later in the season, a splash of purple flowers will make chartreuse foliage come alive (contrast).

In the combos shown here, the white flowers of a White Jacob's ladder match the white edges of a 'Patriot' hosta, creating harmony, while the purple flowers of the 'May Night' salvia create exciting contrast with the chartreuse foliage of the 'Citronelle' heuchera. Imagine if both the hosta and the heuchera were generic green plants. When the Jacob's ladder and salvia went out of bloom, both combinations would be somewhat dull.

'Patriot' hosta and white Jacob's ladder

'Citronelle' heuchera and
'May Night' salvia

Interesting foliage keeps the show going when flowering plants go out of bloom. Choose flowering plants that will highlight the foliage around them, and vice versa.

Using Color Effectively

Speaking of an exciting combo like purple and chartreuse, let's talk a little about the color wheel. It's a handy tool for choosing colors that will create just the kind of feeling you're aiming for in a planting. There is so much that can be said about using the color wheel in garden design, but let's keep it super-simple for our purposes.

The color wheel is a graphic that shows the relationships between colors. It makes it easy to create either harmony or contrast, and differing degrees of each, by combining colors based on the distance between them on the color wheel.

Analogous colors, like yellow and orange, are close to each other on the color wheel. Combining them creates reassuring harmony. The closer two colors are to each other on the color wheel, the more harmonious they are together. Daylilies are a good example to illustrate this. A combo of a red daylily and an orange daylily is more harmonious than one of a red daylily and a yellow daylily. The farther apart two colors are on the color wheel, the more you move into the realm of contrast.

Complementary colors, like purple and yellow, are across from each other on the color wheel. Combining them creates exciting contrast. The farther two colors are from each other on the color wheel, the more contrast they generate. For example, a combo of blue and orange is the ultimate contrast, while a combo of blue and magenta is a little less in-your-face. The closer two colors are on the color wheel, the more you move into the realm of harmony.

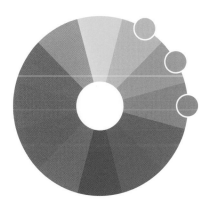

Analogous colors

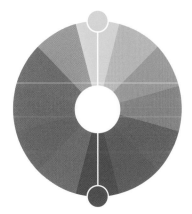

Complementary colors

Analogous colors, when combined, create calm and harmony. Complementary colors, when combined, create excitement and contrast.

Hues, Tints, Shades, and Tones

So we know the basic dozen or so colors on the simple color wheel, but how do we get colors like burgundy, pale pink, sky blue, and mauve? To do that, we bring black and white into the mix.

A pure color is called a hue. Add white to that color, like when you add white to red to make pink, and you've created a tint. Add black to a hue, and you've made a shade. Add both black and white (gray) to a hue, and you've made a tone. Tints are less intense than their original hues, while shades are more intense. Tones can make a color either more or less intense depending on how much black or white is added.

Tints, tones, and shades are fun to play with, especially if you love a single color like purple.

A garden full of pure purples would get overwhelming pretty quickly. But add in some pale lavender flowers and some deep eggplant foliage, and you've created subtle contrast while maintaining the harmony. What you've done is called a color echo.

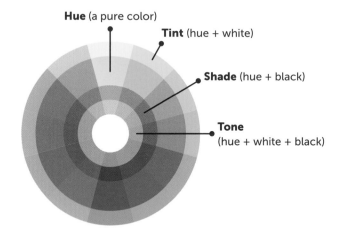

Hue (a pure color)

Tint (hue + white)

Shade (hue + black)

Tone (hue + white + black)

Color Echoes

Creating a color echo is one of easiest and most effective ways to play with color in a planting. For example, the Japanese painted fern shown here is a gorgeous mix of silvery green fronds with deep, dark purple-red midribs. Placing a deep, dark purple-red 'Black Scallop' bugleweed at its base makes a color echo — a perfect pairing. Nestling in a third plant with *light* purple-red blooms, like striped bloody cranesbill geranium, sends this color echo to another level.

Use hues, tints, shades, and tones to create sophisticated combos of plants with similar base hues.

The Psychology of Color

You can use colors in tricky ways to manipulate how you and your visitors feel in your garden.

Warm colors, like red, orange, and yellow (think fire and sunlight), suggest heat and excitement. They stand out and get noticed in a garden. They're the first colors you see at a glance. If you love to throw rousing, exciting parties in your garden, warm colors are the way to go.

Cool colors, like green and blue (think forest and ocean), are soothing and relaxing. They recede into the background of a garden, and tend to be quieter and less noticeable, but no less beautiful. If you think of your garden as your own personal retreat, you might lean toward cool colors.

You can manipulate how relaxing or exciting your planting is by shifting your color scheme back and forth on the color wheel, or by adding contrasting color here or there to mix things up a bit. If you have a passion for pink and tend to lean toward flowers in all of its shades, try throwing in a bit of yellow from the other side of the color wheel to spice things up. That touch of heat and contrast will prevent your pink garden from being too monochromatic and bland.

If you like a multipurpose, well-rounded garden, you'll want to experiment with various colors and their many tints, tones, and shades, to achieve a balanced mix of harmony and contrast. That gives you lots of exciting plant options to play with!

Attention-grabbing warm colors, such as yellow, orange, and red, are energetic and exciting.

Subdued cool colors, such as green, blue, and purple, are calm and reassuring.

What About Black and White?

In the world of plants, white and silver usually count as cool colors (think ice). For example, 'Jack Frost' Siberian bugloss, with its green leaves glazed with silver, looks as if it's been frosted with ice. Oakleaf hydrangea's massive white flower heads look like hefty snow cones. There's something about the purity of white that brings to mind cool cleanliness.

Black, on the other hand, doesn't register as either warm or cool, even though most "blacks" are actually very dark reds or purples. Black does, however, lend lots of excitement and drama! It's a wonderful contrast to just about any plant, and since most botanical blacks come in the form of foliage (besides the odd black-flowered tulip or columbine), they're useful for breaking up the inevitable sea of green that most gardens lean toward.

In a garden, white reads as a cool color, while black can be either warm or cool. Both are dramatic additions to any combination of plants.

And Green?

In a garden, green is almost out of play. It's the neutral hue, because it's everywhere. Like a pale beige wall, it's the backdrop against which colorful foliage and flowers (the artwork) can play. But green doesn't have to be dull. There are so many different greens to work with! Plus, once you add texture and form to the mix, everything gets more interesting.

Texture

Texture is an important element of planting design, but it often is not as carefully considered as color. Big bold leaves, frilly ferny leaves, and everything in between — they all play a part in making a planting dynamic and interesting. A garden full of similar textures reads as a flat composition. Imagine a bed filled with only hostas. Even if you love hostas, it's great at first glance, but you'll get bored pretty quickly. Those hostas are a lot more interesting when interspersed with some strappy leaves, skirted with a shiny groundcover, or accompanied by finely textured or airy perennials. A healthy dose of contrast makes each plant shine.

Most gardens display too much of an in-between texture. This is hard to avoid, since a majority of plants have an in-between texture, but mixing in some with more or less texture prevents a planting from being a bland sea of monotony. Texture can be considered on a few levels.

Leaf Sheen

Leaf sheen is the close-up level of texture. Think of one of your favorite plants. Are its leaves shiny? Rough? Fuzzy? Smooth? Matte? Pleated? Each leaf type reflects light in different ways. European wild ginger has incredibly smooth, shiny leaves and reflects light

dramatically. You can almost see the sunlight glinting off its surfaces. A bit of sheen is especially useful in shady corners, which benefit from light being thrown around a bit.

The flip side would be lamb's ears, which has fuzzy leaves that attract fingers like a magnet. Leaf sheen is more than the way a leaf looks; it's about how it feels to the touch, too. Crocosmia has finely pleated leaves with a medium sheen: not shiny, but not matte, either. The pleats play with light in intriguing ways, using it to make microshadows, if you will. Plants like these beg you to touch them, to run your fingers over their tactile patterns. A mix of sheens is exciting and beckons you closer to revel in the differences.

The sheen of a plant's leaf is a fascinating aspect of texture. It urges you to touch and manipulates light in interesting ways.

Leaf and Flower Size and Shape

The intermediate level of texture is size and shape, both in leaves and flowers. Let's start with leaves. Hostas generally have relatively large, smooth-edged, lance-shaped leaves. A hosta is one of the easiest plants to use when playing with texture, since its beefy foliage is unique in the plant world. Most garden plants have smaller leaves, and lots of them. Planting many small-leaved plants together quickly becomes messy, and otherwise lovely plants lose their individuality, so that you barely notice them as you walk by.

To prevent that kind of garden snooze fest, plant a small-leaved plant with a large-leaved hosta to make both plants stand out, even if they are the exact same colors. Note, however, that if both of plants have a similar leaf shape, the combo can still miss the mark. The lesson here is that it's more important to strive for contrast with texture than it is to create harmony.

Imagine mixing a little bluestem grass with an 'Elijah Blue' blue fescue grass. One has long, blue-green blades, while the other has shorter, thinner blue-green blades. Yes, we've mixed leaf sizes, but those leaves are so similar that the plants get lost in each other — too much harmony.

Mix that little bluestem grass with a 'Silver Mound' wormwood, whose silvery green leaves are similar in color to the bluestem's, and you've mixed leaf shapes and sizes for a much more exciting monochromatic combo.

Leaf sizes and shapes offer lots of opportunities for exciting contrast. However, leaves that are too similar in both can blend into one another boringly.

Leaves that have contrasting sizes and shapes always look more interesting together, even if they're the same color.

The same principle applies to flower shapes and sizes. Mix them up as well to avoid a tame, overly harmonious effect. When flower shapes are too similar, your planting will begin to look like a collection of every color you can find of one plant rather than a thoughtfully planned and engaging composition.

If you've ever seen a bed full of daylilies in many different colors, you get the picture. Lots of flowers, yay! But, hmm, kind of monotonous after a while. The blossoms are all the same relative shape and size. Deep orange 'Primal Scream', yellow 'Happy Returns', and pink 'Rosy Returns' all have the same basic flower shape. They almost get lost in each other, even though their colors are distinct.

Mixing different flower shapes and sizes allows each flower to stand out and shine without competition from similar companions. The disc-and-ray flowers of the purple coneflower, the trumpet-shaped flowers of the 'Happy Returns' daylily, and the flower spires of tiny 'Caradonna' salvia are vastly different, creating enough contrast that each one gets equal individual attention. This combo holds your attention longer, doesn't it?

It's especially important to create contrast when combining flower shapes. This group of daylilies offers a riot of color but is confusing to look at.

A similar mix with different flower shapes makes each individual plant stand out.

Plant Structure

This aspect of texture skirts dangerously close to form, which we'll talk about soon, but it's a little different. Structure refers to how dense a plant is, and how its stems and flowers interact with other plants.

For example, a hosta (it always goes back to hostas, doesn't it?) with big leaves forms a dense mass that either acts as a solid background for other plants when it's behind them or as a blocking screen when it's in front of them. Below, 'Halcyon' hosta blocks the lower foliage of 'Visions in White' astilbe with its dense texture.

On the other hand, 'Big Blue' sea holly, with its loose stems of spiky blue flowers, allows the chartreuse foliage of 'Worcester Gold' blue-beard behind it to shine through.

But that's not all. Structure also refers to the way a plant grows. White Culver's root has strongly vertical stems that contrast nicely with the arching, flowing blades of 'Morning Light' miscanthus. Playing with this aspect of structure gives a planting movement. It makes the eye follow the garden's darting and flowing lines in an exciting way.

Hosta and astilbe

Bluebeard bush and sea holly

Culver's root and miscanthus

Use plant structure to manipulate how people experience a planting. Dense plants block views, drawing you through the garden to see what's behind them. Airy plants can act as a breezy scrim for other plants to peek through beguilingly.

Form

Plants come in all shapes and sizes: tall and skinny, big and round, short and ground-hugging — you name it! A mix of all these shapes and sizes is necessary to make a dynamic, interesting planting. An easy way to see and understand form is to squint your eyes when you look at a plant, so that it's out of focus. Without the distraction of details, you can observe the plant's basic size and shape.

When you blur or shade out the details, you can see that the 'Color Guard' yucca is rounded and spiky, the ostrich fern is upright and vase-shaped, and the Mexican feather grass is fountain-shaped. The distinctions may seem obvious without the blur, but you'd be surprised how much this squinting technique can help you. It focuses your attention on the overall shape of a plant, helping you choose good companions.

As with texture, it's more important to create contrast with plant forms than it is to create harmony. The grouping of three heucheras on the following page shows this concept. They have wildly different colors, but they have similar shapes and sizes. So while the mix of colors is exciting (if a bit chaotic), the planting lacks contrast in form.

An easy way to grasp a plant's form is to squint your eyes, blurring out the details to reveal its overall shape.

Take away the heucheras but one — say 'Citronelle', which has the characteristically mounded shape of a heuchera — and add an upright and larger, blocky, and linear plant like 'Caesar's Brother' Siberian iris. Isn't that so much better? But don't go overboard: Start with one shape and then add contrasting shapes in other sizes. Maybe mix in a similar shape in a contrasting size as well. The general rule is to put large shapes in the back of a planting and to place smaller and smaller shapes as you move toward the front of a bed. But rules are meant to be broken! Every once in a while, slot in a larger shape among a section of lower plants to mix things up.

As with texture, it's more important to create contrast than harmony with plant forms. Even if a grouping of similarly shaped plants looks pleasing, like the heuchera on the left, it can usually benefit from the addition of a contrasting form, such as a clump of iris.

Using the Golden Ratio

Having trouble combining forms and sizes in ways that work? Take a cue from a formula that's been used by architects, designers, and artists since ancient times, and by Mother Nature for eons. Long considered the most pleasing ratio to employ, the golden ratio is an incredibly useful tool for getting a design right the first time. Using the ratio 1:1.618, choose your first plant, determine its mature height, and multiply that number by 1.618 to find the height of a larger plant that would be pleasing next to it.

Keep in mind that plants don't stay the same size once they're installed, like buildings and drawings do, so your perfect golden ratio may change over time. But it's a good start and a neat trick!

A × 1.618 = B

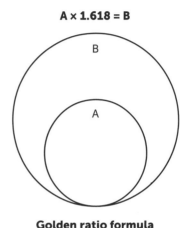

Golden ratio formula

30" × 1.618 = 48.5"

Ostrich fern = 48.5"

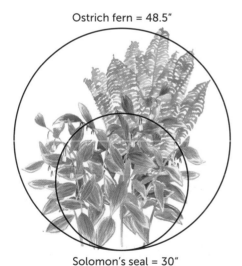

Solomon's seal = 30"

For example, variegated Solomon's seal is 30 inches tall. 30 × 1.618 = 48.5 inches. So you are searching for a companion for your Solomon's seal that is roughly 4 feet tall. Ostrich fern fits the bill!

36" ÷ 1.618 = 22.25"

Peony = 36"

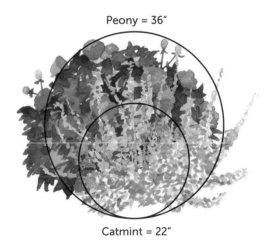

Catmint = 22"

The golden ratio works in the other direction, too. For example, 'Karl Rosenfield' peony generally grows to 3 feet tall. Dividing 36 inches by 1.618 gives you 22.25 inches, or about 2 feet. Pair that peony with a 2-foot-tall 'Walker's Low' catmint for a combo with a guaranteed pleasing proportion.

Take It Over the Top with a Focal Point

Focal points are essential for a compelling planting design. They catch the eye and keep it, inducing you to stop and consider their surroundings. Plants can act as focal points if they are significantly distinct in color, form, or texture from the plants around them — real *wow!* plants — but inanimate objects like birdbaths, sculptures, birdhouses, and even big rocks or a gorgeous urn can do the trick, too, and sometimes even better than a plant.

It doesn't have to be a $1,000 piece of art. Look through your garage, barn, or shed and let your creative juices flow. Have an old bicycle you don't ride anymore? Paint the entire thing bright purple and plop it in the middle of a bed. The compliments will roll in! An interesting focal point establishes the starting point for viewing a garden. So if your planting is lacking one plant that catches the eye, try adding something completely different.

Below is a great combo of ostrich fern, 'Frances Williams' hosta, and Rozanne hardy geranium, but it could use a little something extra. The addition of a large colorful pot adds extra visual oomph. The pot will likely be the first element of this garden people will notice. Then they'll notice the gorgeous planting you've created around it.

Sometimes a focal point such as a colorful urn is all a planting needs to be perfect. Go with your gut, and have fun experimenting.

Designing a Planting

So how do you get started? Well, the easiest way is to pick a plant you like and build off of it. But first you need to pull together a collection of plants to work with. The most basic way to whittle down all of the plants available to you is to decide whether you're designing for full sun, partial shade, or, less often, full shade. Once you make that determination, you can start choosing plants.

1

Determine your light level.

2

Choose a palette of all-season plants.

3

Create a foundation planting.

4

Choose a palette of flowering accent plants.

5

Mix and match until you're pleased with the results.

BONUS

Add a focal point.

1
Sun or Shade?

It's not easy to define the amount of sun a garden bed receives, and many areas of your garden may straddle the line between two designations. Trial and error is definitely a factor when choosing plants for those areas. But here are some general guidelines for determining your starting point.

Full sun, in the horticultural world, means at least 8 to 10 hours of direct sunlight a day. Preferably these hours include the early-afternoon hours, when sunlight is at its most intense. If a plant that prefers full sun doesn't get enough, it may not grow as strongly, and it may get leggy as it reaches for more light. It might flop over. It might not flower well, or at all. If it's a perennial, it probably won't survive more than a couple of years before giving up the ghost.

Partial shade is a simplified term that can mean many things. It could refer to morning sunlight and afternoon shade (maybe on the eastern side of a house or wall), to an area where a plant gets less than four hours of direct sunlight (preferably not in the heat of the afternoon), or to the edge of a woodland or the dappled sunlight under a tall tree. There is a big range of shade requirements in the plant world, and these requirements should be considered when designing a planting.

Full shade is just what it sounds like — no direct sunlight at all. This could be an area in the midst of a woodland garden, on the north side of a house or wall, and so on. Your plant choices in these situations are limited, unfortunately. But there are options out there if you're willing to do the research and suffer through some experimentation.

2
Choose a Palette of All-Season Plants

All-season plants (ASP) are those that catch the eye all season long due to their unusual foliage color, fantastic texture, striking form, or all-season flowers. Most are planted mainly for their attractive foliage, though flowers may appear at some point in the season. A select wonderful few, like some shrub roses, ENDLESS SUMMER hydrangeas, and 'Walker's Low' catmint, can flower on and off all season. Every planting should comprise enough all-season plants that it can carry its weight for months on end without the benefit of flowering accent plants (that's Step 4). Ideally, your ASPs include a mix and match of colors, forms, and textures that create a tapestry upon which the fleeting flowers you do add can shine.

From the stickers, select a number of all-season plants that appeal to you and are appropriate for the level of sunlight you've chosen. Be sure to include plants in a wide variety of colors, textures, and forms. Choose many more plants than you think you'll need so you can mix and match easily without going back for more. For this example, let's design a full-sun planting using the 13 plants shown here, selected from the full collection of stickers. Yes, it's a *lot* of plants! But it will be fun to whittle them down.

A note about using the stickers and the worksheets: The plants are drawn to scale based on mature growth habit. As you arrange them, using either the grid work surface or the garden scene, place them fairly close together to approximate the final result. When you actually plant a new garden, you'll need to space the plants out to accommodate their growth over the several months or even years.

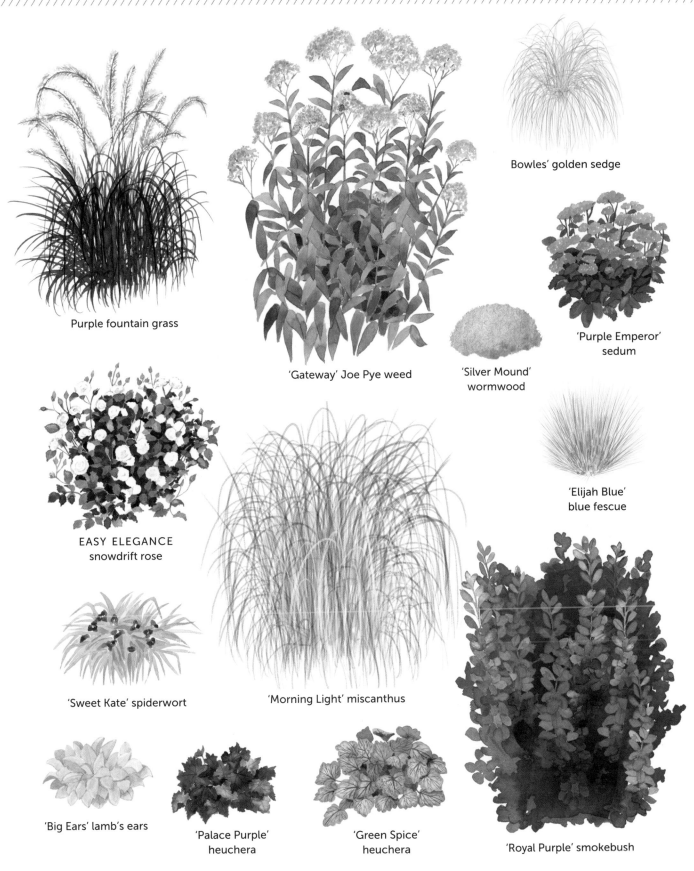

Purple fountain grass

'Gateway' Joe Pye weed

Bowles' golden sedge

'Silver Mound' wormwood

'Purple Emperor' sedum

EASY ELEGANCE snowdrift rose

'Elijah Blue' blue fescue

'Sweet Kate' spiderwort

'Morning Light' miscanthus

'Big Ears' lamb's ears

'Palace Purple' heuchera

'Green Spice' heuchera

'Royal Purple' smokebush

3 Arrange the All-Season Plants

▶ **Choose one plant** from the group that you really like and pull it forward. Let's begin with 'Royal Purple' smokebush, a gorgeous shrub with long stems of rounded, deep burgundy leaves. It's got great texture and form, and the color is dreamy.

◀ **Start adding plants** around it. Choose companions that both contrast and harmonize with your base plant, in a variety of shapes, sizes, colors, and textures. The tall, dark, and handsome smokebush makes a great background plant. It begs for something bright in front of it, so let's add a light-colored, fountain-shaped 'Morning Light' miscanthus!

▶ **The miscanthus is so beautifully silvery** — let's look for something to echo it. The Snow-drift rose, with its white blooms all summer (a long-flowering all-season plant — the holy grail!), would complement it nicely, as would a 'Big Ears' lamb's ears.

◀ **The burgundy is visually receding now** — dark colors do that. Let's bring it forward with a similar color placed toward the front. A 'Palace Purple' heuchera works, as does a 'Purple Emperor' sedum, so let's add both. The sedum blooms in late summer and fall, but its deep purple foliage looks dramatic and wonderful all season, hence its all-season plant status.

◀ **A two-toned collection has emerged.** It looks great together, and would be just fine on its own, but let's choose a few flowering accent plants to dress it up a bit!

4
Choose a Palette of Flowering Accent Plants

Flowering accent plants (FAPs) are grown primarily for their flowers. Since most of these plants are perennials, their blossoms typically last a few weeks at most. When not in flower, FAPs are by no means ugly or boring. True, they may not capture lots of attention or add dramatic interest to the overall bed or border. But their foliage makes a great filler among the plants that do grab the eye.

For that reason it's important to consider the foliage of a flowering accent plant, especially its texture and form. One well-chosen FAP can significantly change the way a planting looks.

This step should be a little more purposeful than Step 2. Keeping the color wheel in mind, choose flowers that can relate to both the all-season plants you've selected for your planting *and* your goals for the planting. Aim for plants that flower at various times within the season, so that you'll have something blooming almost continuously. In this example, the Snowdrift rose does some of the flowering work for you. The sedum covers late summer and early fall.

Below is a palette of 10 flowering plants chosen from the sticker collection that both contrast and harmonize with the all-season plants we arranged in the previous step.

Yellow is opposite purple on the color wheel, which makes it perfect for adding exciting contrast to the dark purple foliage in the arrangement. 'Zagreb' Threadleaf coreopsis, 'Coronation Gold' yarrow, and 'Happy Returns' daylily would all work for this purpose.

The big white flowers of a 'Casa Blanca' Oriental lily would brighten things quite a bit, and also echo the white blooms of the Snowdrift rose.

Pink and purple flowers would create a color echo with the dark purple foliage plants in the all-season plant combo. Here we show anise hyssop, purple coneflower, striped bloody cranesbill geranium, 'Caesar's Brother' Siberian iris, blazing star, and 'Marshall's Delight' bee balm.

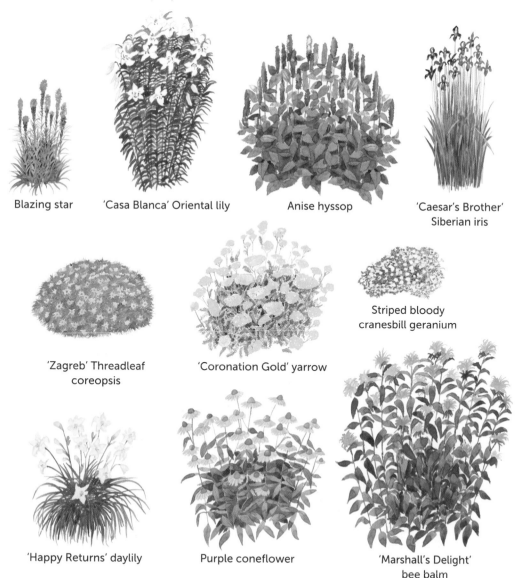

Blazing star   'Casa Blanca' Oriental lily   Anise hyssop   'Caesar's Brother' Siberian iris

Striped bloody cranesbill geranium

'Zagreb' Threadleaf coreopsis   'Coronation Gold' yarrow

'Happy Returns' daylily   Purple coneflower   'Marshall's Delight' bee balm

5
Add Flowering Accent Plants

With your all-season plant palette established, start playing with the flowering accent plant stickers. Put them in, pull them out, and rearrange as needed to make things fit and look just right together. Eliminate any plants that don't work. Again, keep seasonality in mind. Most of the flowering accent plants are illustrated at their peak, when flowering. But perennials flower at varying times, and for limited periods, so consider bloom time when envisioning your garden in real life.

The main reason why all-season plants should be your first priority is that they can carry a planting through the entire season. The more flowering accent plants you add, the more of a snapshot in time you're creating. The key is to use FAPs to create little highlights throughout the season. So don't overdo it on the flowers!

▼ Our first try is shown below. We've added a 'Casa Blanca' Oriental lily next to the Snowdrift rose, and then a blazing star, a Purple coneflower, and a 'Happy Returns' daylily in other areas of the planting. It's looking good, but a bit unbalanced. All of the silver/white plants are on one side. We need to distribute them better.

▶ This is a little better. We've moved the 'Casa Blanca' Oriental lily to the other side, ditched the blazing star, and moved the Purple coneflower to the middle. But there's always room for improvement. Now the Oriental lily looks too bold and doesn't seem to fit. Plus, once those lily blooms are finished, they leave a gap in interest. We also need something else behind the 'Morning Light' miscanthus. It is wispy and would benefit from being sited in front of a dense background plant.

▶ In this version, we've taken out the 'Casa Blanca' Oriental lily and moved the rose to that spot. The rose will bloom on and off all season and won't overpower its neighbors with overly bold texture. The 'Gateway' Joe Pye weed, another all-season plant from our original group, is a good background for the miscanthus. It doesn't bloom until late summer, but until then it's a great textural, deep green backdrop. The flowers, when they do appear, match the rest of the planting beautifully.

BONUS
Add a Focal Point

This step is optional. If you feel your design is done, leave it alone! But if it's missing something, and another plant just won't do, then consider adding a focal point. If your planting leans toward mounded shapes, think about adding a linear object, like a birdhouse on a pole. If your planting has many vertical elements, try something rounded, like a large rock or big urn. If there's a lot of green going on, try a bold and colorful ornament. These are just suggestions; use your imagination!

Start adding and subtracting objects until you find one that immediately feels right — it might be an item you don't expect to work. Perhaps you even discover that two focal points look great. But be careful. There's nothing worse than a garden cluttered with objects that distract from the beauty of the plants. A focal point should enhance the planting, not dominate it. You may find that the more you play with focal points, the more you realize that the planting is just right without one. Trust your gut!

So it looks like we're done! The flowering accent plants are fairly well distributed among the all-season plants so that they don't create large pockets of less-interesting foliage when they're not in bloom. There should be something in bloom for most of the season, especially with the inclusion of the Snowdrift rose and 'Happy Returns' daylily, which both bloom on and off all season. When the Purple coneflower isn't blooming, its clean green foliage holds its own and contrasts nicely with the nongreen foliage around it. Pretty good!

But we don't have to be done . . . Keep tinkering if you'd like, taking things out, adding things in. It might be nice to incorporate some early spring-blooming plants to extend the planting's interest, for example. Or maybe you prefer an earlier version of the design, before we really shuffled it. That's okay, too! Want to keep going? Begin adding plants to either side of the design to start building a full-fledged border!

Meet the Plants

The plants we've selected are popular, reliable, and readily available. They are separated into two categories: all-season plants to form the foundation of a design and flowering accent plants to highlight and enhance. But these categories should be considered fluid. Feel free to reinterpret a plant as you see fit. You may absolutely love the foliage of a flowering accent plant, and want to highlight it. Perfectly fine! You may find an all-season plant's foliage boring, but you love its flowers. Also perfectly fine!

We've listed all the plants alphabetically on the facing page for quick reference, but within each category on the following pages, **the plants are listed from large to small**. Each has a brief description of growth habit, light requirements, and so on.

ALL-SEASON PLANTS

(ALPHABETICAL LIST)

Autumn Snakeroot, 'Black Negligee' (p. 49)

Black Mondo Grass (p. 60)

Blue Fescue (p. 60)

Bluebeard, 'Worcester Gold' (p. 50)

Bugleweed (p. 61)

Cardoon (p. 47)

Catmint (p. 53)

Elephant Ears (p. 45)

Feather Reed Grass, 'Karl Foerster' (p. 45)

Fern, Christmas (p. 55)

Fern, Japanese Painted (p. 58)

Fern, Northern Maidenhair (p. 57)

Fern, Ostrich (p. 46)

Hardy Geranium, Rozanne (p. 56)

Heuchera (p. 53)

Hosta (p. 52)

Hydrangea, ENDLESS SUMMER (p. 46)

Hydrangea, Oakleaf (p. 43)

Japanese Forest Grass (p. 57)

Japanese Maple (p. 40)

Joe Pye Weed (p. 42)

Lady's Mantle (p. 52)

Lamb's Ears (p. 56)

Little Bluestem (p. 50)

Lungwort (p. 58)

Mexican Feather Grass (p. 54)

Miscanthus (p. 44)

Ninebark (p. 41)

Pigsqueak (p. 56)

Purple Fountain Grass (p. 48)

Purple Smokebush (p. 40)

Rose, Ever-Flowering Shrub (p. 48)

Sage, Garden (p. 59)

Sedge (p. 51)

Sedum, Creeping, 'Angelina' (p. 61)

Sedum, Upright (p. 54)

Siberian Bugloss (p. 55)

Solomon's Seal, Variegated (p. 51)

Spiderwort, 'Sweet Kate' (p. 57)

Spirea, 'Ogon' (p. 47)

Spotted Deadnettle (p. 60)

Wild Ginger, European (p. 61)

Wormwood, 'Silver Mound' (p. 59)

Yellow Wax Bells (p. 49)

Yucca (p. 50)

FLOWERING ACCENT PLANTS

(ALPHABETICAL LIST)

Anise Hyssop (p. 64)

Astilbe (p. 77)

Baptisia (p. 63)

Barrenwort (p. 78)

Bee Balm (p. 66)

Begonia, Hardy (p. 76)

Black-Eyed Susan (p. 69)

Blazing Star (p. 72)

Bloody Cranesbill Hardy Geranium, (p. 78)

Cardinal Flower (p. 73)

Columbine (p. 75)

Coneflower (p. 65)

Coreopsis (p. 76)

Crocosmia (p. 64)

Daylily (p. 67)

Goat's Beard (p. 62)

Iris, Bearded (p. 67)

Iris, Siberian (p. 70)

Jacob's Ladder (p. 74)

Masterwort (p. 73)

Oriental Lily (p. 63)

Peony (p. 68)

Phlox, Garden (p. 69)

Phlox, Woodland (p. 77)

Russian Sage (p. 66)

Salvia (p. 70)

Sea Holly (p. 71)

Shasta Daisy (p. 71)

Small Globe Thistle (p. 75)

Turtlehead (p. 65)

White Culver's Root (p. 62)

Yarrow (p. 74)

Yellow Foxglove (p. 72)

ALL-SEASON PLANTS

Plants are listed by size. For an alphabetical list, see page 39.
For Zone information, see Resources, page 79.

Japanese Maple

Acer palmatum cultivars

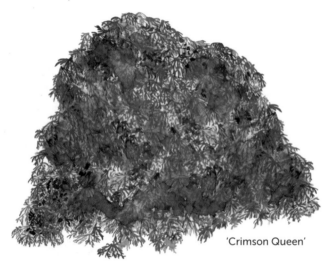

'Crimson Queen'

Deciduous trees, hardy in Zones 5–8

SIZE: Up to 15 feet tall and wide

PREFERS: Full sun/partial shade

Japanese maples make most gardeners' hearts beat faster. Their intriguing leaves and sinuous branches are mesmerizing, and they are instantly calming. They can be upright and spreading, small and mounding, or gently weeping. For smaller gardens, the weeping thread-leaf form of 'Crimson Queen' is a great choice. It can't help but be a stately focal point. Its deep red leaves have a wonderfully fine texture, and depending on how it's pruned, it can have either an airy or dense structure.

Purple Smokebush

Cotinus coggygria cultivars

'Royal Purple'

Deciduous shrubs, hardy in Zones 5–8

SIZE: Up to 12 feet tall and wide

PREFERS: Full sun

FLOWERS: Summer

A purple smokebush makes a big impact on a planting. Its deep, dark foliage is vigorous, dense, and bold, while its delicate, cloudlike summer blooms add a contrasting touch of airiness. The shrub makes a wonderful backdrop for less-dramatic perennials, making them more exciting than they could ever be on their own. Smokebushes love to be cut back hard in early spring, after which they will send out long, strong stems of fresh new foliage. If managed in this manner, most smokebushes max at out 7 to 8 feet tall each year.

Ninebark

Physocarpus opulifolius cultivars

'Dart's Gold'

COPPERTINA

Deciduous shrubs, hardy in Zones 3–7

SIZE: Up to 10 feet tall and 15 feet wide

PREFERS: Full sun

FLOWERS: Early summer

Ninebarks are incredibly useful shrubs. They are dense with a medium leaf texture, and they grow in dramatically dark colors. Although the original green version is still around, it's not very exciting. While the white, domed spring flowers are a wonderful bonus, this plant is really all about the foliage. The most popular ninebark in the past several years has been DIABOLO, which flaunts dark foliage and grows quite big. But in recent years, new, more compact varieties have been introduced, as well as some exciting chartreuse- and copper-hued options like 'Dart's Gold' and COPPERTINA.

Joe Pye Weed

Eupatorium spp. and cultivars

'Gateway'

Deciduous perennials, hardy in Zones 3–7

SIZE: Up to 7 feet tall and 4 feet wide

PREFERS: Full sun/partial shade

FLOWERS: Mid- to late summer

Joe Pye weeds are stunning North American natives that can be found on wildflower-bedecked roadsides of the eastern United States, though they are suitable for gardens across the country. Their towering stems of rough, dark green leaves are topped in late summer with massive domes of mauve flowers that attract butterflies in droves. 'Gateway' is a moderately sized option that grows 5 or 6 feet tall and up to 3 feet wide. Use it as a tall, substantial, vertical background in a garden bed, with the flowers as a bonus.

Oakleaf Hydrangea

Hydrangea quercifolia and cultivars

Deciduous shrubs, hardy in Zones 5–9

SIZE: Up to 6 feet tall and 8 feet wide

PREFERS: Full sun/partial shade

FLOWERS: Midsummer

'Little Honey'

Oakleaf hydrangeas are architectural four-season gems! Their russet peeling branches are beautiful all winter. Their rough, beefy leaves begin their show in spring, starting small but growing and unfurling like big hands until they cloak the shrub, overlapping thickly. This coarse-textured, dense mass of foliage makes a wonderful backdrop for perennials all season long, but the huge white flowers that appear in late summer send this shrub over the top.

The flowers pinken as they age and eventually dry to beige, when they can be cut for everlasting arrangements indoors. The foliage turns brilliant shades of red and purple for a fiery fall show. Just dreamy. If that doesn't quite sell you, or if an 8-foot-wide shrub seems intimidating, there's a golden-foliaged, dwarf variety, 'Little Honey'!

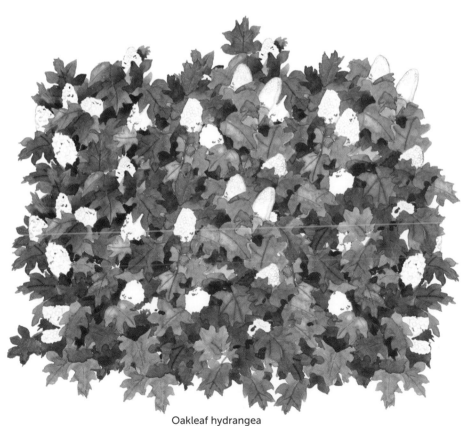

Oakleaf hydrangea

Miscanthus

Miscanthus sinensis cultivars

'Cosmopolitan'

'Morning Light'

Deciduous grasses, hardy in Zones 5—9
SIZE: Variable, up to 6 feet tall and wide
PREFERS: Full sun
FLOWERS: Fall

Miscanthus are a large group of ornamental grasses available in a wide range of sizes, textures, colors. They form large clumps quite quickly, and are a steady, reliable presence in a garden. When the wind blows, they billow and gently rustle. They make a wonderful backdrop for bolder-textured, darker-leafed perennials, and their late-summer plumelike blooms are a wonderful bonus. Keep in mind, though, that clumps of miscanthus must be divided every few years to keep looking their best, and it's a big job!

Perhaps the most famous and popular miscanthus is 'Morning Light'. Its long, thin, arching blades are green striped with white, which, because of the plant's fine, wispy texture, translates as silvery green. Varieties with wider variegated blades, such as 'Cosmopolitan', are more obviously green and white.

'Karl Foerster' Feather Reed Grass

Calamagrostis × acutiflora 'Karl Foerster'

Deciduous grass, hardy in Zones 5–9

SIZE: Up to 6 feet tall and 2 feet wide

PREFERS: Full sun

FLOWERS: Midsummer to fall

Possibly one of the most useful and famous of the ornamental grasses, 'Karl Foerster', once it blooms in midsummer, forms a strongly vertical column that acts almost like a pillar in a planting, but with a fine texture. The blooms and the foliage fade to beige and then buff in fall, and may even look good through the winter, if not smashed by snow, before they must be cut back to make way for fresh foliage in spring.

Elephant Ears

Colocasia esculenta cultivars

'Black Magic'

Tender perennials, hardy in Zones 9–11

SIZE: Up to 5 feet tall and wide

PREFERS: Partial shade

Elephant's ears aren't hardy in most areas of the country, so they need to be dug up and stored indoors for winter, but the effort is worth it for the bold, tropical texture they lend to a planting in partial or bright shade. The leaves do, indeed, remind one of an elephant's ear, and they come in lots of colors, sizes, and patterns. You'll almost always be able to find 'Black Magic' (it lives up to its name) in a good garden center, but do keep an eye out for more options — you'll soon be addicted.

Ostrich Fern

Matteuccia struthiopteris

Deciduous perennial, hardy in Zones 3–8

SIZE: Up to 5 feet tall and 3 feet wide

PREFERS: Partial shade

Ostrich ferns are no shy woodland creatures. They're big and bold yet finely, uniformly textured. They form a wonderful mass of visually cooling foliage, spreading over time into large swaths. They are invaluable as a backdrop to ephemeral perennials, and they fill space wonderfully when many woodland plants are flagging mid- to late summer.

ENDLESS SUMMER **Hydrangea**

Hydrangea macrophylla 'Bailmer'

Deciduous shrub, hardy in Zones 6–9

SIZE: Up to 4 feet tall and 5 feet wide

PREFERS: Full sun/partial shade

FLOWERS: All season

Bigleaf hydrangeas are traditional favorites. These shrubs, with their big, bodacious blooms in either pink or blue, depending on your soil acidity, are magnetic! They evoke summers in Nantucket and sprawling summer cottages by the ocean. Older traditional varieties only bloom for a short time, but ENDLESS SUMMER is a superstar, blooming all season long. Since its introduction, more all-season-bloomers have become available, but ENDLESS SUMMER keeps plugging along and is a sure find in your local nursery.

'Ogon' Spirea

Spiraea thunbergii 'Ogon'

Deciduous shrub, hardy in Zones 5–8

SIZE: Up to 4 feet tall and 5 feet wide

PREFERS: Full sun

FLOWERS: Spring

Most spireas are perfectly nice shrubs, but once their blooms are gone for the season, their fine green foliage fades into the background a bit. Not so with 'Ogon'. It blooms early in spring, its white flowers appearing on long, arching stems before its leaves appear. Then the fine, feathery foliage emerges, at first gold and then transitioning to chartreuse as the summer heats up. In fall it often turns brilliant orange and is slow to lose its leaves, often hanging on to them until Christmas. This is a true all-season star.

Cardoon

Cynara cardunculus

Deciduous biennial in Zones 7–9, though usually grown as an annual

SIZE: Up to 4 feet tall and wide

PREFERS: Full sun

FLOWERS: Summer

Cardoon isn't hardy in many areas of the country, but, like elephant's ears, it's worth the effort to plant it each year, because it forms a dramatic mound of big, beefy, jagged leaves in a stunning silvery gray. Where hardy, it will produce big, purple, thistlelike flowers its second year, though if started from seed indoors and planted out as a good-sized seedling in spring, it might flower the first year. Bonus: cardoon's leaf stalks are edible and taste like artichokes when cooked! This makes sense, as the plant is closely related to the commercially produced artichokes you buy in the grocery store.

Purple Fountain Grass

Pennisetum setaceum 'Rubrum'

**Deciduous grass, hardy in Zones 9–10,
usually grown as an annual**

SIZE: Up to 4 feet tall and wide
PREFERS: Full sun
FLOWERS: Summer

Purple fountain grass is a classic plant for containers, where its burgundy blades and brown flowers serve as a dramatic centerpiece. But when grown in the ground, it gets even bigger! It has a fine texture, but with its density and color, it has a bold presence. Pick up an extra one up when you shop for your petunias in spring and put it in the ground. It will start blooming early and keep going all summer, its flowers dancing in the breeze.

Ever-Flowering Shrub Rose

Rosa cultivars

Deciduous shrubs, hardy in Zones 5–9

SIZE: Up to 4 feet tall and wide
PREFERS: Full sun
FLOWERS: All season

Roses have a reputation for being fussy and hard to grow. Not so, if you choose wisely! There are lots of roses now that are more disease resistant and that rebloom all season. For a small planting, choose an easy-care shrub rose like CAREFREE WONDER or a rose from the KNOCK OUT series or the EASY ELEGANCE series.

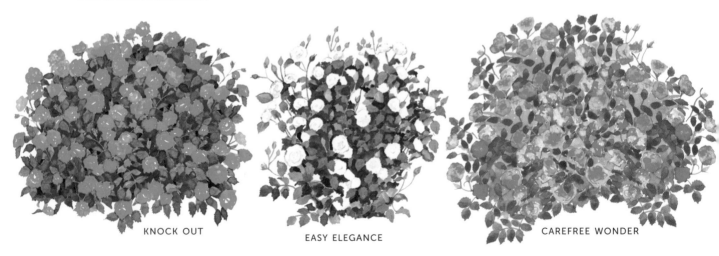

KNOCK OUT   EASY ELEGANCE   CAREFREE WONDER

Yellow Wax Bells

Kirengeshoma palmata

Deciduous perennial, hardy in Zones 5–8

SIZE: Up to 4 feet tall and 3 feet wide

PREFERS: Partial shade

FLOWERS: Late summer

You won't find this shade lover in many gardens, but when you do, you'll want to take it home with you. Yellow wax bells grows into a big clump of arching, upright stems cloaked densely in matte, medium-textured, jagged-edged green leaves. In late summer, when most woodland perennials have long stopped blooming, yellow wax bells flaunts pale yellow buds and bell-shaped flowers that rise above the foliage on dark stems. It's wonderful!

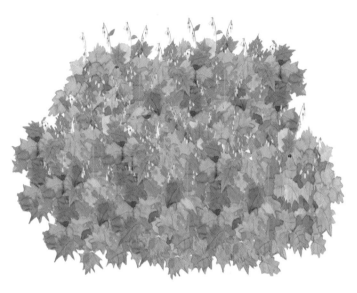

'Black Negligee' Autumn Snakeroot

Actaea simplex 'Black Negligee'

Deciduous perennials, hardy in Zones 4–8

SIZE: Up to 4 feet tall and 2 feet wide

PREFERS: Full sun/partial shade

FLOWERS: Early fall

Most autumn snakeroots are unassuming green plants for most of the season until fall, when tall flowering stems shoot up, soon to be topped by long, bright bottlebrushes of tiny white flowers. But dark-foliaged varieties like 'Black Negligee' (try 'Hillside Black Beauty', too) are even better, because their foliage draws attention all season long and makes even more of a contrast with its white flowers. Use it to create drama against green perennials, and mix it with purple flowers for a great color echo.

'Worcester Gold' Bluebeard

Caryopteris × clandonensis 'Worcester Gold'

Deciduous shrub, hardy in Zones 6–9

SIZE: Up to 3 feet tall and 5 feet wide

PREFERS: Full sun

FLOWERS: Late summer

This bright shrub brings sunshine into your garden. Its fine-textured foliage forms a more loosely textured golden mound against which pink, blue, and purple flowers positively pop. In fall, its bright blue flowers do just that, and they linger for weeks to make wonderful additions to late-season bouquets.

Yucca

Yucca filamentosa and cultivars

Evergreen perennial, hardy in Zones 5–10

SIZE: Foliage up to 3 feet tall and 5 feet wide

PREFERS: Full sun

FLOWERS: Midsummer to late summer

'Color Guard'

Yuccas, with their stiff, spiky blades, are wonderfully architectural. Combine them with loose perennials with small flowers for an incredible contrast in texture. Yellow-variegated varieties like 'Bright Edge' and 'Color Guard' are even more fun to play with. Combine them with yellow flowers for a great color echo, and with red or purple for exciting contrast.

Little Bluestem

Schizachyrium scoparium and cultivars

Deciduous grass, hardy in Zones 5–9

SIZE: Up to 3 feet tall and 2 feet wide

PREFERS: Full sun

FLOWERS: Summer

Little bluestem is a U.S. native prairie grass that has made its way into gardens for its stiffly upright, dense tuft of blades that vary in color from powder blue to medium green. Wispy blooms appear in late summer, and as fall arrives the flowers' puff to buff-colored seed heads and the blades turn shades of orange and burgundy. Gorgeous! As a vertical plant with fine texture, it combines beautifully with mounding plants.

Variegated Solomon's Seal

Polygonatum odoratum 'Variegatum'

Deciduous perennial, hardy in Zones 4–8

SIZE: Up to 3 feet tall, spreading to up to 3 feet wide or more

PREFERS: Partial shade/full shade

FLOWERS: Late spring

Variegated Solomon's seal is a classic, can't garden-without-it plant for shade. Purchasing it in the nursery is a bit discouraging, because it often looks piddly, with only a couple of straggly stems. But buy it anyway. Take it home, put it in the ground, and watch it spread. Each year it will get bigger and better, forming a thick patch of individual arching stems (all pointing in the same direction) with leaves that have the perfect amount of cream feathering along their edges. In late spring, small but bright green-and-white tubular flowers dangle, sometimes in pairs, in a line along the undersides of the stems. In fall the foliage turns warm gold. Pair this architectural plant with frilly ferns for contrast.

Sedge

Carex spp. and cultivars

Deciduous and evergreen perennials, hardy in Zones 5–9

SIZE: Up to 28 inches tall and 20 inches wide

PREFERS: Full sun/partial shade

Bowles' golden sedge

'Ice Dance'

If you love ornamental grasses but you have partial shade, sedges will fill the void! They can take full sun or partial shade and come in a big range of colors and looks, all with a fountainlike form and fine texture. The golden and variegated varieties are fun and brighten dark, damp corners. Bowles' golden sedge grows up to 28 inches tall and 20 inches wide and is pure, bright gold, while 'Ice Dance' sedge has green blades striped with cream that read as silver from a distance. 'Ice Dance' is also a bit smaller, growing to 18 inches tall and wide. But don't stop with these two! There are also beautiful bronze varieties.

Hosta

Hosta spp. and cultivars

'Liberty'

'Patriot'

'Halcyon'

'Elegans'

'Sun Power'

'Frances Williams'

'Sum and Substance'

Deciduous perennials, hardy in Zones 3–8

SIZE: Varies significantly, from a few inches to 4 feet tall and as wide, or wider

PREFERS: Partial shade

FLOWERS: Early summer

Hostas are the most popular shade plant ever cultivated. There are hundreds and hundreds of cultivars — in oodles of combinations of size, color, and form, from pale chartreuse to powder blue to deep green, many with exciting variegations, and from tiny miniatures to behemoths 4 feet tall and even wider. Every shade garden needs at least a dozen or two. Their bold forms and textures are a welcome contrast to the majority of shade plants that have subtler, finer textures.

Most hostas are grown for their foliage alone, and some gardeners even cut the flower stalks as they emerge to keep the focus on the luscious leaves. But a few hostas, like 'Elegans', have wonderfully showy blooms that are worth keeping. Some are even fragrant. If you decide to cut the blooms, they make wonderfully long-lasting and unexpected additions to bouquets, as do the leaves themselves.

Lady's Mantle

Alchemilla mollis

Deciduous perennial, hardy in Zones 4–7

SIZE: Up to 2 feet tall (in bloom) and 3 feet wide

PREFERS: Full sun

FLOWERS: Late spring to fall

Lady's mantle is a classic cottage-garden plant with soft mounds of blue-green, round, ruffly, scalloped leaves topped sporadically through the season with clouds of delicate, bright chartreuse flowers. Its medium texture and versatile color go with almost every plant you can think of! It goes especially well, though, with purple flowers. Pair it with a salvia for a great color and form contrast.

Catmint

Nepeta spp. and cultivars

Deciduous perennial, hardy in Zones 4–8

SIZE: Up to 2 feet tall and 3 feet wide

PREFERS: Full sun

FLOWERS: Summer

'Walker's Low'

Catmints are workhorses! Their rough, gray-green foliage forms exuberant mounds that are topped with loose spires of deep lavender flowers in late spring and early summer, and sporadically afterward if the plant is trimmed after the first flush of flowers. In fact, with its similar foliage and flowers, catmint is an easier-to-grow alternative to lavender. Its foliage is aromatic, and its flowers attract bees, hummingbirds, and butterflies.

Catmints are exceptionally drought tolerant, and deer and rabbits don't care to munch on them. 'Walker's Low' is an especially popular and robust variety, but not as low as the name implies — it grows up to 30 inches tall! Pair catmint with yellow daylilies or coreopsis for a surefire winning combo.

Heuchera

Heuchera spp. and cultivars

Deciduous perennials, hardy in Zones 3–8

SIZE: Up to 2 feet tall and wide

PREFERS: Full sun/partial shade

FLOWERS: Summer

'Palace Purple'   'Citronelle'   'Caramel'

'Green Spice'   'Red Lightning'   'Obsidian'

Heucheras (also known as coral bells) are some of the most versatile and useful foliage plants around. They come in a wide range of leaf colors, from olive green to the deepest burgundy, many with silver markings that make them shimmer in shade or sunlight. They're invaluable for creating color contrast in a green-heavy garden. While they're grown mainly for their bold mounds of foliage, their wands of small, early-summer flowers are charming, too.

Mexican Feather Grass

Nassella tenuissima

Deciduous grass, hardy in Zones 7–10

SIZE: Up to 2 feet tall and wide

PREFERS: Full sun

Imagine a soft, tawny ponytail growing out of the ground and you've pictured Mexican feather grass. Its hair-fine, silvery green blades and pale buff blooms form a billowing, graceful, flowing fountain that is downright irresistible. You won't be able to stop yourself from running your hands through this grass's tresses. As good as it feels, it looks even better in the garden. Its fine texture and gossamer translucence makes it a perfect companion to a multitude of plants. While well-behaved in many areas of the country, in some areas, especially in some parts of California, Mexican feather grass can spread itself about annoyingly. Ask around before choosing it for your garden.

Upright Sedum

Sedum spp. and cultivars

Deciduous perennials, hardy in Zones 3–10

SIZE: Up to 2 feet tall and wide

PREFERS: Full sun

FLOWERS: Fall

Sedums are tough, drought tolerant, and beautiful, with upright stems of thick, green, succulent leaves topped with flat domes of mostly pink or purple flowers in fall. The most famous of them is 'Autumn Joy', with green leaves and mauve flowers, but also check out deep, dusky purple-leaved varieties like 'Purple Emperor' that are stunning all season long, even before their mauve flowers appear.

'Autumn Joy'   'Purple Emperor'

Christmas Fern

Polystichum acrostichoides

Evergreen perennial, hardy in Zones 3–8

SIZE: Up to 18 inches tall and 3 feet wide

PREFERS: Partial shade/full shade

Christmas fern is an eastern U.S. native that's tough and easy to grow. Its leathery, deep green fronds grow in a dense fountain shape and slowly expand into hefty clumps. It might not have lots of bells and whistles, but this fern is a true stalwart, a steadfast companion to more ephemeral woodland plants. Bonus: it's evergreen in most gardens! Pair it with hefty hostas and light green foliage for contrast that will make this deserving fern stand out.

Siberian Bugloss

Brunnera macrophylla cultivars

Deciduous perennial, hardy in Zones 3–7

SIZE: Up to 18 inches tall and 24 inches wide

PREFERS: Partial shade/full shade

FLOWERS: Spring

'Jack Frost'

Siberian bugloss might remind you of a forget-me-not in spring: its tiny, light blue flowers are similar, and just as charming. But rather than fade into obscurity after flowering, these plants keep wowing all season with spectacular foliage. One of the most famous and readily available (and beautiful) varieties is 'Jack Frost'. Jack has big, heart-shaped dark green leaves broadly overlaid with a silvery white (with the green veins showing through in an intricate pattern) that shimmers in the shade. Pair it with a silvery Japanese painted fern for a stunning color echo, or maybe with a deep green Christmas fern to highlight its deep green veins. Both ferns lend great textural contrast.

Rozanne Hardy Geranium

Geranium 'Gerwat'

Deciduous perennial, hardy in Zones 5–8

SIZE: Up to 18 inches tall and 24 inches wide

PREFERS: Full sun/partial shade

FLOWERS: Late spring to fall

Most hardy geraniums fall into the flowering accent plant category. After their flowers are spent, their foliage is nothing exciting. But Rozanne, possibly the most famous hardy geranium ever, flowers for months on end, making it an all-season plant! Its loose stems sprawl along the ground, and its purple flowers weave in and out of other plants seamlessly until it's hard to know where the geranium begins and ends.

Lamb's Ears

Stachys byzantina and cultivars

Deciduous perennial, hardy in Zones 4–8

SIZE: Up to 18 inches tall (in bloom) and
   24 inches wide

PREFERS: Full sun

FLOWERS: Early summer

'Big Ears'

Lamb's ears forms a carpet of furry, bright silver foliage that begs to be touched. Its taller, fuzzy stems of early-summer purple flowers are beautiful, but without prompt deadheading they can make the plant look messy. New cultivars are broader-leafed and dense, and look great all season long. 'Big Ears' (often sold as 'Helene von Stein') is one of the best and one of the easiest to find. It's a little greener and less felted, so it combines gracefully with other plants, and it rarely flowers. Contrast is key with this plant: pair it with dark green and burgundy foliage and bright blooms for the biggest impact.

Pigsqueak

Bergenia cordifolia cultivars

Evergreen perennial, hardy in Zones 3–8

SIZE: Up to 16 inches tall and 24 inches wide

PREFERS: Full sun

FLOWERS: Early spring

Such a funny name for a plant, isn't it? Best guess is that if you rub this plant's broad, rubbery, evergreen leaves between two fingers just right, they squeak. Name aside, this plant is great for adding beefy texture to an otherwise lacy planting. It forms substantial clumps over time that make an effective ground cover, and its stems of medium pink spring flowers are quite showy. Most pigsqueaks also turn brilliant shades of bronze in fall and winter.

Northern Maidenhair Fern

Adiantum pedatum

Deciduous perennial, hardy in Zones 3–8

SIZE: Up to 16 inches tall and wide

PREFERS: Partial shade

Lacy, delicate, and magical: northern maidenhair fern is all three. Its fronds float on black, wirelike stems, making fans of light green foliage that shoot out from a central coil. The plant spreads steadily to form a thick patch, never losing its overall fine texture that mixes with hostas stunningly. You might spot this distinctive fern on rambles along shady country roads, as it's a U.S. woodland native.

'Sweet Kate' Spiderwort

Tradescantia 'Sweet Kate'

Deciduous perennial, hardy in Zones 5–9

SIZE: Up to 16 inches tall and wide

PREFERS: Full sun/partial shade

FLOWERS: Summer

'Sweet Kate' is the spiderwort that put spiderworts on the map. While all spiderworts are lovely, with thick clumps of green, grassy foliage and white, pink, or blue flowers, 'Sweet Kate' features foliage in a shocking shade of chartreuse, with bright purple-blue flowers that are positively electric against it. Each flower lasts for only one day, but plenty more replace it, for up to eight weeks in early summer to midsummer. Try mixing this stunner with broad-leafed perennials to highlight its strappy leaves.

Japanese Forest Grass

Hakonechloa macra cultivars

Deciduous perennial, hardy in Zones 5–9

SIZE: Up to 15 inches tall and 2 feet wide

PREFERS: Partial shade

'Aureola'

The gracefully weeping, golden chartreuse foliage of Japanese forest grass looks like a bright waterfall flowing through a shady garden. It's a wonderful plant that you cannot have too much of. It lights up the shade with a hue that complements every neighbor. While 'Aureola' is the gold standard, with bright yellow blades narrowly striped with green, also try the aptly named 'All Gold' and any number of new varieties, such as 'Beni-Kaze', that mix in hints of burgundy. Japanese forest grass, with its gentle mounds of foliage, begs to be paired with more upright perennials and with bolder texture.

Japanese Painted Fern

Athyrium niponicum var. *pictum*

Deciduous perennial, hardy in Zones 5–8

SIZE: 12 to 16 inches tall, spreading slowly to form a patch 2 feet wide

PREFERS: Partial shade/full shade

Possibly the most popular plant in the shade section of the nursery (besides hostas, of course), Japanese painted fern is low to the ground but not easily missed. The bright, silvery gray-green fronds are adorned with a central stripe of deep, dark, iridescent reddish purple that is darkest at the stem and fades as it moves toward the edges. The gently curving fronds shoot out from the center of the clump in a starburst, making this plant quite striking on its own or in combination with plants with deep purple foliage or pink flowers.

Lungwort

Pulmonaria spp. and cultivars

'Excalibur'

'Mrs. Moon'

Deciduous perennials, hardy in Zones 4–8

SIZE: 12 inches tall and up to 24 inches wide

PREFERS: Partial shade/full shade

FLOWERS: Spring

Lungworts are just as coveted for their showy leaves as they are for their purple and pink spring flowers. It's an essential foliage plant for shady gardens. Most lungworts, like 'Mrs. Moon', have low rosettes of medium green leaves with bright silver spots, though some varieties, like 'Excalibur', have an even stronger wash of silver that makes the plant shine in shade. There are tons of variations to explore and choose from. Pair lungworts with hostas for a similar form and leaf shape in a different size, or with ferns for a nice texture, form, and color contrast.

Garden Sage

Salvia officinalis and cultivars

Evergreen woody perennial, hardy in Zones 6–8

SIZE: Up to 1 foot tall and 2 feet wide
PREFERS: Full sun
FLOWERS: Early summer

Sage is often overlooked as an ornamental plant and relegated to the herb garden. But its gray-green, silvery leaves form a tidy, ever-expanding mound of foliage that reflects light beautifully and pairs well with any number of plants. 'Berggarten' has broader leaves than the common variety, giving it a pumped-up texture and tidier appearance. 'Purpurascens', the purple sage, has a flush of dusky purple to its leaves that is subtle but beautiful and lends itself to purple pairings. This isn't a typical perennial: don't cut it down after the leaves drop in fall. Wait until spring to carefully prune it, and it will reward you with lush new growth each year.

'Purpurascens'

'Berggarten'

'Silver Mound' Wormwood

Artemisia schmidtiana 'Silver Mound'

Evergreen perennial, hardy in Zones 5–8

SIZE: Up to 1 foot tall and 2 feet wide
PREFERS: Full sun

'Silver Mound' is the perfect name for this plant! It positively shimmers in the sunlight, and it forms a creeping cushion of feathery, fine-textured, aromatic foliage — a bonus because you can't resist touching it. This great edging plant prefers poor soils and is deer resistant and drought tolerant, too. Mix 'Silver Mound' with vibrant flowers and maybe spiky foliage for contrast. Purple foliage is a great companion, too, such as 'Purple Emperor' sedum or 'Obsidian' heuchera.

Blue Fescue

Festuca glauca and cultivars

Evergreen grass, hardy in Zones 4–8

SIZE: Up to 12 inches tall and wide

PREFERS: Full sun

'Elijah Blue'

Blue fescue looks like silvery blue powder puffs when dotted around a garden. Its unique color is ideal for making exciting contrasts within a planting. It is drought tolerant and, in mild climates, may be evergreen. The most popular variety is 'Elijah Blue', which forms perfect tight domes of thin, icy blue blades. Tall, buff-colored blooms appear in midsummer. You can enjoy them or trim them back to maintain the grass's tidy appearance. Blue fescue is a no-brainer for combinations with white flowers, and it looks great with peach, too. Yarrow fits the bill perfectly.

Spotted Deadnettle (a.k.a. Lamium)

Lamium maculatum cultivars

Deciduous perennial, hardy in Zones 4–8

SIZE: Up to 8 inches tall, spreading up to 3 feet wide

PREFERS: Partial shade/full shade

FLOWERS: Summer

'White Nancy'

This old-fashioned ground cover is just as loved now as it was decades ago, but newer varieties are more fun! Spotted deadnettle creeps to form a large patch of small, triangular leaves that's wonderful for filling space in a shady garden. At just 8 inches tall, it makes a great carpet below taller shade plants. In summer the pink- to purple-flowering spikes are beautiful. The most popular varieties are heavily marked with silver. 'White Nancy' is a prime example, with leaves that are almost completely silver and bright white flowers that truly light up the plant, even in full shade.

Black Mondo Grass

Ophiopogon planiscapus 'Nigrescens'

Evergreen perennial, hardy in Zones 6–10

SIZE: Up to 8 inches tall and 12 inches wide

PREFERS: Full sun/partial shade

So much drama in such a small package! This tiny grassy plant is as close as you can get to black in the plant world. It grows in low tufts that spread slowly to form small patches and is stunning paired with silver-leaved plants. While blooms appear in summertime, you might not even notice the tiny lavender flowers. It really is all about that black foliage.

Bugleweed

Ajuga reptans cultivars

Evergreen perennial, hardy in Zones 3–9

SIZE: Up to 6 inches tall, spreading to form a carpet up to 3 feet wide

PREFERS: Partial shade

FLOWERS: Late spring

'Black Scallop'

The original form of bugleweed is considered a pest, invading lawns so completely that your only option is to start over from scratch to get rid of it. But modern varieties are better-behaved and wonderfully colorful and textural ground covers. They spread to form a tight, low carpet of puckered leaves 2 to 3 inches tall, at most. In spring their taller spikes of showy purple flowers are a welcome sight, but the foliage is still the star. The variety 'Black Scallop' is especially attractive, with broad, dark purple, almost black crinkled leaves. and dark purple flowers.

'Angelina' Creeping Sedum

Sedum rupestre 'Angelina'

Deciduous perennial, hardy in Zones 6–9

SIZE: Up to 6 inches tall and 24 inches wide

PREFERS: Full sun

FLOWERS: Summer

Unlike upright sedums that stand up to 2 feet tall, this creeping evergreen sedum forms low mounds of bright gold to chartreuse needle-like foliage just 6 inches tall. The color is fabulous: the perfect skirt of light for a multitude of companions. 'Angelina' loves sun and will spread quickly if happy. It's drought tolerant, and in fall the tips of the stems turn shades of orange.

European Wild Ginger

Asarum europaeum

Evergreen perennial, hardy in Zones 4–8

SIZE: Up to 3 inches tall and 12 inches wide

PREFERS: Partial shade/full shade

FLOWERS: Late spring, but they are not showy

Given time, this beguiling little perennial forms a low, tight carpet of rounded, shiny, ground-hugging leaves in the deepest of greens. Plant several at once to form a large patch more quickly. It makes a wonderful ground cover, the perfect canvas upon which ephemeral woodland flowers can play.

FLOWERING ACCENT PLANTS

Plants are listed by size. For an alphabetical list, see page 39.

Goat's Beard

Aruncus dioicus

Deciduous perennial, hardy in Zones 3–7

SIZE: Up to 6 feet tall and 4 feet wide

PREFERS: Partial shade/full shade

FLOWERS: Early summer to midsummer

A wonderful but underused U.S. native plant for shady gardens, goat's beard has frilly, ferny leaves and bright sprays of white flowers up to an astonishing 6 feet tall. Like an astilbe on steroids, its flowers are large for a shade-loving plant — a welcome contrast to the delicate, ephemeral flowers shady gardens tend toward. Plant this beauty toward the back of a border, and give its foliage a bold-textured companion, like a big hosta or two.

White Culver's Root

Veronicastrum virginicum and cultivars

Deciduous perennials, hardy in Zones 3–8

SIZE: Up to 6 feet tall and 3 feet wide

PREFERS: Full sun

FLOWERS: Midsummer to early fall

This North American native has a strongly vertical habit that is a good foil for more common mounding plants. Its organized whorls of dark green leaves and delicate, spirelike flowers stand out in a crowd. The plants spread to form tidy clumps that can be divided and added to other garden beds, lending a strong sense of cohesion to an overall garden. While plant breeding has produced some interesting colors, the white form is the easiest to find and work with.

Baptisia

Baptisia australis and cultivars

Deciduous perennial, hardy in Zones 3–9

SIZE: Up to 5 feet tall and 3 feet wide

PREFERS: Full sun

FLOWERS: Early summer

This unusual plant looks more like a shrub than a perennial. It forms a tall upright, rounded mass of tidy blue-green leaves that are topped by spires of pretty, medium blue, pealike flowers, followed by decorative, dusty black seedpods. It is native to the United States and, because of its deep taproot, is quite drought tolerant. It doesn't mind poor soils, either. Lots of new varieties are available now, with bronze flowers, yellow flowers, and more, but the original blue is still pretty darned wonderful. Some gardeners may need to stake this plant to keep it from flopping — a peony support works perfectly — but in most gardens it's tough enough to stand on its own.

Oriental Lily

Lilium cultivars

'Stargazer'   'Casa Blanca'

Deciduous perennials, hardy in Zones 4–8

SIZE: Up to 5 feet tall and 2 feet wide;
plant in groupings for larger masses

PREFERS: Full sun

FLOWERS: Summer

Oriental lilies make gardeners swoon. They're the biggest bang for your buck. Just plant a five-pack of bulbs from the garden center and you'll be rewarded with 5-foot-tall stems topped with the biggest, most fragrant, beautiful flowers you've ever seen. You'll be able to see and smell them from 30 feet away. There are tons of colors to choose from, but start with the two most famous varieties: pure white 'Casa Blanca' and hot pink and white 'Stargazer'. Plant a few extra off to the side to cut and bring indoors, where they'll fill your home with sweet scent.

Anise Hyssop

Agastache foeniculum and cultivars

Deciduous perennial, hardy in Zones 6–10

SIZE: Up to 4 feet tall and wide

PREFERS: Full sun

FLOWERS: Midsummer to early fall

Another great North American native, anise hyssop makes a hefty clump of upright stems of light green leaves that smell like a pleasant mix of mint and licorice when rubbed between your fingers (this makes the plant deer resistant, too!). Closely related to mint, anise hyssop is vigorous but not a nuisance, even when it self-sows. Bees, hummingbirds, and butterflies love the cylindrical lavender flower spikes, which are edible. Pair this plant with something equally robust, perhaps with a rounder form.

Crocosmia

Crocosmia spp. and cultivars

Deciduous perennials, hardy in Zones 6–9

SIZE: Up to 4 feet tall and wide

PREFERS: Full sun

FLOWERS: Midsummer

'Lucifer'

Crocosmias are ravishing! Each plant forms a clump of upright, strappy leaves that are heavily pleated to the point of fascination. If that weren't enough, in midsummer the flowers appear on long stems atop which a zigzaggy row of buds open from top to bottom. The tubular flowers can be any shade of yellow, orange, or red, but the most popular variety, by far, is 'Lucifer', which is a brilliant scarlet. Pair it with other hot colors and with shorter plants that will showcase its fountainlike form.

Turtlehead

Chelone spp. and cultivars

Deciduous perennial, hardy in Zones 3–8

SIZE: Up to 4 feet tall and 3 feet wide

PREFERS: Full sun/partial shade

FLOWERS: Late summer

This U.S. native forms thick stands of dark green leaves topped with stout spikes of sturdy flowers that really do look like a turtle's head with its mouth open. While the texture of the leaves is average, it's not easy to locate something of this height and density for a shady garden, so it's a snap to find contrasting companions. You'll most often see the medium pink variety 'Hot Lips' in your local garden centers, though you might also find the white form, *C. glabra*.

'Hot Lips'

Coneflower

Echinacea purpurea and cultivars

Deciduous perennials, hardy in Zones 3–9

SIZE: Up to 4 feet tall and 3 feet wide

PREFERS: Full sun

FLOWERS: Midsummer to early fall

Perhaps the most ubiquitous perennial garden staple ever, coneflowers are tough and beautiful. These U.S. natives bloom prolifically, make wonderful cut flowers, and multiply year after year. Their colors seem to go with everything. It's a must-have plant that you should not garden without. There are many variations, but the original purple coneflower is most popular and white forms like 'White Swan' are also gorgeous.

Purple coneflower

'White Swan'

Bee Balm

Monarda spp. and cultivars

Deciduous perennials, hardy in Zones 4–9

SIZE: Up to 4 feet tall and 3 feet wide

PREFERS: Full sun

FLOWERS: Midsummer to late summer

Bee balm is an old-fashioned perennial that is just as beloved now as it was decades ago. It is long-blooming with cheerful, rosy flowers that attract bees and hummingbirds in droves. Plant this medium-textured staple in the middle of a border, where it will form a larger and larger clump each year that you can divide to spread about the garden or share with friends.

'Jacob Cline'   'Marshall's Delight'

Russian Sage

Perovskia atriplicifolia and cultivars

Deciduous perennials, hardy in Zones 6–9

SIZE: Up to 4 feet tall and 3 feet wide

PREFERS: Full sun

FLOWERS: Late summer

Russian sage is as cool as a cucumber in hot, dry gardens. The combination of its silvery gray-green, finely textured leaves and sprays of tiny violet flowers is unlike any other plant. Russian sage is strongly upright and linear, great for combining with mounding plants, and the aromatic foliage is deer resistant. It blooms for several weeks in summer and is quite drought tolerant. Wait until spring to cut back its dead stems. Leaving them in place for winter helps the plant survive the cold.

Bearded Iris

Iris cultivars

'Dusky Challenger'

'Beverly Sills'

'New Moon'

'Immortality'

'Victoria Falls'

'Variegata'

Deciduous perennials, hardy in Zones 3–9

SIZE: Up to 4 feet tall and 2 feet wide

PREFERS: Full sun

FLOWERS: Early summer

Bearded irises are like potato chips. With so many colors to choose from, you can't have just one! Their fans of stiff foliage and tall stems of big, flamboyant flowers are wildly popular and widely available. Honestly, it's like having a paint palette in your hand. What color do you need to make your planting exactly so? There's an iris that'll work. It's impossible to pinpoint the best ones, so try lots! But for something a little different, check out the popular cream-variegated bearded iris (*I. pallida* 'Variegata'), which looks interesting before and after it blooms.

Daylily

Hemerocallis spp. and cultivars

'Primal Scream'

'Happy Returns'

'Siloam Double Classic'

'Rosy Returns'

Deciduous perennials, hardy in Zones 3–10

SIZE: Up to 3 feet tall and wide

PREFERS: Full sun

FLOWERS: Late spring to late summer

Wildly popular daylilies come in a rainbow of warm colors. While each colorful bloom lasts only one day, there are always more to take its place. Sprinkle them throughout your garden, weaving their strappy leaves in among courser-textured plants to fill in blank space. With thousands of colors and shapes to choose from, some with broader leaves and some with spidery flowers or huge, thick-petaled flowers, there's a vast daylily world out there to explore.

Peony

Paeonia spp. and cultivars

Deciduous perennials, hardy in Zones 4–8

SIZE: Up to 3 feet tall and wide

PREFERS: Full sun

FLOWERS: Late spring

Mmm, peonies. Big mounds of lush foliage and huge, extravagant flowers that smell like heaven. It doesn't get any better than when the peonies are in bloom. Traditional herbaceous peonies are the standard. They're lush and beautiful and come in every shade of white, pink, and warm red. Their foliage may begin to decline before fall — they're definitely spring and early-summer stars.

Tree peonies last longer, have bigger but fewer flowers, and maintain a woody framework over the winter, but they're harder to grow. A new group of peonies called intersectional or Itoh peonies are a mix of herbaceous and tree peonies. They flop less in rain, have bigger flowers in more colors, and last longer than herbaceous varieties, and they're easier to grow than tree peonies and tidily die back to the ground for winter.

'Sarah Bernhardt'

'Bartzella' (Itoh)

'Festiva Maxima'

'Karl Rosenfield'

'Kopper Kettle' (Itoh)

Garden Phlox

Phlox paniculata cultivars

Deciduous perennials, hardy in Zones 4–8

SIZE: Up to 3 feet tall and 3 feet wide

PREFERS: Full sun

FLOWERS: Summer

Old-fashioned garden phlox is so feminine and pretty. While the mass of foliage it makes is the epitome of average and is often plagued by powdery mildew (although there are many great mildew-resistant varieties), its domes of five-petaled summer flowers, most often in shades of white and pink, are adorable and sweetly fragrant. Use this plant as a generic foliage filler, with the flowers as the prize.

'David'

'Robert Poore'

Black-Eyed Susan

Rudbeckia spp. and cultivars

Deciduous perennials, hardy in Zones 4–9

SIZE: Up to 3 feet tall and wide

PREFERS: Full sun

FLOWERS: Late summer to fall

This beloved plant's nondescript foliage won't get much notice until late summer, but when it blooms, black-eyed Susan is the star of the garden and a sure sign that fall is just around the corner. Its dark-eyed, daisylike flowers are a rich golden yellow that positively glows. When the petals drop and the garden starts to succumb to winter, the seed heads that are left behind are attractive, too, to both humans and birds.

Mix this classic with some grasses that will contrast with its form and texture in early summer and keep it company with their own flowers in fall. You're guaranteed to find the most popular variety, 'Goldsturm', in almost any nursery. But once you buy a black-eyed Susan, you'll likely never have to buy another. They moderately seed themselves, making them a popular giveaway plant.

'Goldsturm'

Salvia

Salvia spp. and cultivars

'May Night'

'Caradonna'

Deciduous perennials, hardy in Zones 5–9

SIZE: Up to 3 feet tall and 2 feet wide

PREFERS: Full sun

FLOWERS: Varies, from early summer to fall

There are so many salvias in the world that it's hard to know where to begin, but they're all incredibly tough, adaptable plants with colorful flowers that span the rainbow. There are lots of annual and tender perennial varieties, but for perennial gardens, 'Caradonna' and 'May Night' are the most popular. They're both compact varieties with spires of blue-purple flowers, but 'May Night' has beefier foliage and brighter flowers, while 'Caradonna' has darker, narrower flower spikes with dramatic black stems. Their thin flower spikes are perfect for pairing with rounder flowers like those of perennial geraniums or daylilies, or with the mounding foliage of a heuchera.

Siberian Iris

Iris sibirica cultivars

'Caesar's Brother'

Deciduous perennials, hardy in Zones 4–9

SIZE: Up to 3 feet tall and 2 feet wide

PREFERS: Full sun/partial shade

FLOWERS: Early summer

Siberian irises are the more-refined cousins of the flamboyant bearded irises. Their thin, strongly upright blades make a strong vertical mass, serving as the perfect backdrop for mounding perennials. Their flowers, usually in shades of purple but also available in white and yellow, top the stems in early summer and combine beautifully with peonies.

Sea Holly

Eryngium spp. and cultivars

Deciduous perennials, hardy in Zones 5–8

SIZE: Up to 3 feet tall and 2 feet wide

PREFERS: Full sun

FLOWERS: Midsummer to late summer

Sea hollies truly do look like they should grow at the bottom of the ocean. They form rosettes of low-growing spiny foliage and loose, branching stems of flowers. Each head of tiny blue flowers has a showy steel blue, spiky collar. Sea hollies love sun and are tolerant of sandy soils and drought. Fine-textured grasses are perfect companions for showing off sea hollies' awesome hard edges.

'Big Blue'

Shasta Daisy

Leucanthemum × *superbum* cultivars

Deciduous perennials, hardy in Zones 5–8

SIZE: Up to 3 feet tall and wide

PREFERS: Full sun

FLOWERS: Early summer to early fall

Nothing can transport you back to your childhood faster than a daisy, and Shasta daisies are the absolute best of the best. With clean, strong, attractive foliage and long-lasting, bright clean white-and-yellow flowers, this workhorse of a perennial mixes well with other forms, colors, and textures. 'Becky', the classic beloved variety that you'll find in most garden centers, is a sure performer. Shasta daisies expand enthusiastically but not annoyingly. If yours gets a little too big for its allotted space, dig up some clumps from the edges and either find new homes for them or give them away to a lucky friend.

'Becky'

Blazing Star

Liatris spicata and cultivars

Deciduous perennial, hardy in Zones 4–9

SIZE: Up to 3 feet tall and 2 feet wide

PREFERS: Full sun

FLOWERS: Late summer

Upright batons of purple-pink blooms on stems lined with thin, bladelike leaves make this sturdy plant a study in lines. Blazing star is a drought-tolerant sun and warmth lover. Birds, bees, and butterflies adore it, but deer don't. The blooms make excellent cut flowers. In the garden, its upright form and grassy foliage mix well with mounding plants, and its flowers pair beautifully with yellows and golds.

Yellow Foxglove

Digitalis grandiflora

Deciduous perennial, hardy in Zones 3–8

SIZE: Up to 3 feet tall and 18 inches wide

PREFERS: Partial shade

FLOWERS: Early summer to midsummer

Yellow foxglove's lovely spires of hanging, tubular, sunny flowers are wonderful in shade because they shine bright against dark backgrounds. They make a great vertical accent to surrounding mounding plants, and the soft yellow mixes well with almost any other hue. If you cut the flowers back as soon as they're finished, the plant may rebloom in late summer. This species is tougher and lasts longer than any other foxglove, and it self-seeds nicely. Be aware, though, that all parts of the plant are highly toxic to humans if eaten. But it's deer resistant!

Cardinal Flower

Lobelia cardinalis

Deciduous perennial, hardy in Zones 3–9

SIZE: Up to 3 feet tall and 18 inches wide

PREFERS: Full sun/partial shade

FLOWERS: Late summer

This U.S. native loves moist soil and is often found at the edge of woodland streams. If you have a damp spot in your garden, or if you're a fastidious waterer, you'll love cardinal flower. Its spires of scarlet blooms with dark stems are a wonderful vertical element in partial-shade gardens where upright plants are few and far between. Hummingbirds love it!

Masterwort

Astrantia major and cultivars

Deciduous perennial, hardy in Zones 4–7

SIZE: Up to 3 feet tall and 18 inches wide

PREFERS: Partial shade

FLOWERS: Early summer to midsummer

Masterwort is a wonderful shade perennial with little domes of tiny, pale cream to pink flowers skirted by a spiky ruff. You'll have to look closely to see these details, but as a whole, masterwort makes its mark on a shady planting for the brightness of its blooms and for their numbers. The medium-textured, dark green foliage isn't showy, and may not get noticed often when the plant isn't in bloom, but it does make a nice contrast against bright-leaved hostas.

Jacob's Ladder

Polemonium caeruleum and cultivars

Deciduous perennials, hardy in Zones 4–8

SIZE: Up to 3 feet tall and 1 foot wide

PREFERS: Partial shade

FLOWERS: Early summer

Jacob's ladder gets its name from its fernlike leaves composed of slender leaflets lined up along a central stem. The leaves form a dense, fine-textured mass about 1 foot tall, but in early summer the plant shoots up flowering stems up to 3 feet tall topped with little rounded five-petaled flowers in yellow, blue, or white. While the foliage is interesting, it's small enough that it's not exceptionally noticeable among other plants in a larger planting. Except, that is, for the variegated forms which are exciting even when not in bloom, with leaflets edged in wide bands of bright cream.

White Jacob's ladder

Jacob's ladder

Variegated Jacob's ladder

Yarrow

Achillea spp. and cultivars

Deciduous perennials, hardy in Zones 3–9

SIZE: Up to 30 inches tall and wide

PREFERS: Full sun

FLOWERS: Early to late summer

Yarrow is an old-fashioned perennial with lots of variations. Most have silvery green, finely textured, and ferny, aromatic foliage in common, but their flat-topped, dense clusters of tiny flowers come in many subtle colors and color combinations. Of the most popular varieties in garden centers now, 'Apple Blossom' has pale to medium pink flowers all mixed together, while 'Coronation Gold' is, indeed, gold-flowered. 'Terracotta' ranges from pale yellow to orange. Yarrow prefers lean, well-drained soil — it tends to flop in rich soil — and will spread quickly if happy. It attracts butterflies but not deer, and it performs as a wonderful cut flower.

'Coronation Gold'

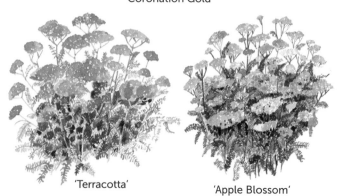
'Terracotta'

'Apple Blossom'

Columbine

Aquilegia spp. and cultivars

Deciduous perennials, hardy in Zones 3–8

SIZE: 18 to 30 inches tall and 16 to 20 inches wide

PREFERS: Full sun/partial shade

FLOWERS: Late spring to midsummer

Columbines come in a veritable rainbow of colors, with constant new variations emerging every year. In fact, if you plant a few in your garden, they might produce babies in colors you didn't plan on but don't mind keeping. Columbine's nodding, spurred, colorful flowers are great for bouquets, where they last for more than a week. Newer varieties, like those in the Origami series, have bigger flowers and longer bloom periods. 'Black Barlow' is a double-flowered variety that is deep, deep mahogany and incredibly dramatic. For a more natural look, go with yellow columbine.

'Black Barlow'

Yellow columbine

'Origami Blue and White'

'Origami Red and White'

Small Globe Thistle

Echinops ritro and cultivars

Deciduous perennial, hardy in Zones 3–9

SIZE: Up to 2 feet tall and wide

PREFERS: Full sun

FLOWERS: Late summer

Small globe thistle is stunning. A bright mound of jagged, gray-green leaves is topped in late summer with gleaming silver stems of spherical, spiky flowers in a cool shade of medium to deep blue. The flowers stand out beautifully against ornamental grasses and pair well with yellow flowers in a different form, perhaps like those of 'Coronation Gold' yarrow. This plant is truly unique, and bees and butterflies love it. It's drought tolerant and deer resistant, too!

Hardy Begonia
Begonia grandis

Deciduous perennial, hardy in Zones 6–9

SIZE: Up to 2 feet tall and 18 inches wide

PREFERS: Partial shade

FLOWERS: Summer

If you love begonias as houseplants, you'll love this hardy perennial begonia for the garden. It forms a thick mound of hefty, matte, lopsided-heart-shaped leaves topped in late summer with drooping sprays of waxy pink flowers on deeper pink stems. The leaves are green on top but have red veins underneath, which shine through to give the leaves a rosy glow. Mix hardy begonia with big-leaved hostas and ferns to add some textural contrast and some late-season pizzazz at a time when not many other shade plants are blooming.

Coreopsis
Coreopsis spp. and cultivars

'Early Sunrise'

'Zagreb'

Deciduous perennials, hardy in Zones 4–9

SIZE: Up to 24 inches tall and 18 inches wide

PREFERS: Full sun

FLOWERS: Varies, and some flower sporadically all season

Coreopsis, also commonly called tickseeds, are cheerful plants with sunny yellow flowers. They're tough and drought tolerant, and many bloom sporadically throughout the season. Threadleaf coreopsis (such as 'Zagreb') forms a round mass of very fine-textured foliage with masses of little yellow flowers, while other coreopsis species have bolder-textured foliage and larger, even double, flowers. All of them benefit from being deadheaded after they bloom to encourage more blooms. The plants are deer resistant and attract butterflies.

Astilbe

Astilbe spp. and cultivars

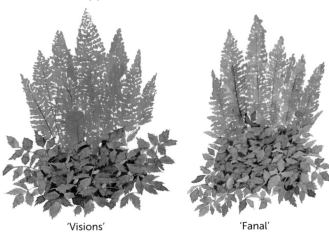

'Visions'   'Fanal'

'Visions in White'

Deciduous perennials, hardy in Zones 4–9

SIZE: Up to 24 inches tall and 18 inches wide

PREFERS: Full sun/partial shade

FLOWERS: Early summer

An indispensable plant for shade, astilbes have been popular forever, for good reason. Their ferny, glossy, dark green foliage looks great all season and makes an excellent ground cover, and their fuzzy plumes of colorful, fine-textured flowers, in all shades of white, pink, peach, magenta, and red, are a welcome sight in summer when not many other shade plants are blooming. The flowers are wonderful in arrangements and can even be dried. Trouble-free and easy to grow, astilbes require moist soil — especially if grown in full sun.

Woodland Phlox

Phlox divaricata and cultivars

Deciduous perennial, hardy in Zones 4–8

SIZE: Up to 14 inches tall and 20 inches wide

PREFERS: Partial shade

FLOWERS: Spring

Garden phloxes (*Phlox paniculata* cvs.) get all the attention, but woodland phloxes are just as wonderful, if a bit more subdued. This U.S. woodland native spreads steadily to form loose mounds of fine-textured, slightly sticky foliage and, in spring, lavender-blue, starry, five-petaled flowers. Butterflies and hummingbirds are attracted to the lightly fragrant flowers. Cut the flower stems back after the flowers are gone to keep the plants tidy.

Barrenwort

Epimedium spp. and cultivars

Deciduous perennials, hardy in Zones 4–9

SIZE: Up to 14 inches tall and 24 inches wide

PREFERS: Partial shade

FLOWERS: Spring

Red barrenwort

'Sulphureum'

Barrenworts, or epimediums, are incredibly tough, great-looking ground covers with layers of stiff, floating leaves on wiry stems. In spring, their clouds of flowers look like little skydivers falling downward, their limbs flung wide. Plant one in your garden and next spring you'll be back at the garden center to buy every other variety you can find. The flowers, while not huge, are incredibly charming, and they make a sophisticated sight in a tiny vase by your powder room sink, where they seem to last forever. You could definitely consider this an all-season plant, too, for its clean, hardworking foliage.

Two of the best and most available barrenworts are the red barrenwort, which has deep pink and pale yellow flowers, and 'Sulphureum' barrenwort, which has bicolored yellow flowers. Both have a showy red tinge to their leaves as they emerge in spring. The leaves usually revert to green for the summer and then deepen to red again in fall. In warmer climates, they may be evergreen.

Bloody Cranesbill Geranium

Geranium sanguineum cultivars

Deciduous perennials, hardy in Zones 4–8

SIZE: Up to 9 inches tall and 16 inches wide

PREFERS: Full sun/partial shade

FLOWERS: Summer

This group of adorable hardy geraniums is incredibly fine-textured, with masses of small leaves that form a mound covered in round, five-petaled magenta flowers, although the striped bloody cranesbill geranium has pale pink flowers with darker pink veins. They bloom mostly in early summer but will rebloom sporadically throughout the summer before the foliage turns attractive shades of red in fall.

'Max Frei'

Striped bloody cranesbill

Glossary of Common Gardening Terms

Annual. A plant that completes its life cycle in one season and does not come back again in spring

Deadhead. To remove the spent flowers from a plant to prevent a plant from going to seed, to encourage the plant to keep flowering, and to make the plant look tidier

Deciduous. Having foliage that dies back in winter, and then reemerges in spring

Evergreen. Having foliage that stays in place all winter

Ground cover. A plant that spreads to cover bare ground, cloaking it with foliage and discouraging weed seeds from sprouting

Hardy. Able to survive the winter in a particular climate

Perennial. A plant that dies back to the ground in winter and reemerges in spring

Self-sow. When a plant goes to seed, and the seeds drop to the ground and sprout readily without any human intervention

Tender perennial. A plant that is perennial only in warm climates, and that is treated as an annual or taken indoors during the winter in cooler climates

Resources

The USDA Plant Hardiness Zone Map
http://planthardiness.ars.usda.gov/PHZMWeb/

The zones on this handy map represent the average lowest winter temperature in each region. Knowing your zone is essential when choosing perennials for your garden. For example, Zone 3 has an average winter low temperature of −40°F. If you live in Zone 3, a plant that is only hardy in Zones 5 and warmer (it will only survive winter temperatures down to −20°F), will likely not survive the winter in your garden. No need to strain your eyes trying to find your town on the map, pretty as it is. Just plug in your zip code and the website will spit out your zone. Voila!

The Missouri Botanical Garden's Plant Finder
www.missouribotanicalgarden.org/plantfinder/plantfindersearch.aspx

This incredible database covers 7,500+ plants, from old favorites to new and exciting species and cultivars. Search by plant name or by the characteristics of a plant to fill a need in your garden. Need a perennial for a shady bed in Zone 4 that's 2 to 3 feet tall with pink flowers? The Plant Finder has 270 suggestions that fit the bill. You'll get detailed descriptions, photos, growing information, and much more information on each plant's dedicated page. So much fun!

University of Minnesota's Plant Information Online
http://plantinfo.umn.edu

Found a plant you simply must have in the Plant Finder but can't find it in your local nursery? This handy website will help you! It represents almost a thousand nurseries, allowing you to find sources for over 80,000 plants! You can also search for references of more than 140,000 plants in garden magazines, books, and scientific literature so that you can research your favorite plants, too. You can even find a list of nurseries in your area and narrow them by specialty. And it's all free!

Gardeny Goodness
www.gardenygoodness.com

Visit the author's website and blog for real-life, in-garden pictures of many of the plants illustrated in this book, and for oodles of inspirational photos and informative articles.

dedicated to Rob and Kaia

The mission of Storey Publishing is to serve our customers by
publishing practical information that encourages
personal independence in harmony with the environment.

Edited by Carleen Madigan and Lisa Hiley
Art direction and book design by Michaela Jebb
Text production by Jennifer Jepson Smith
Cover and interior illustrations by © Scott Jessop
Back cover photography by © Balavan/iStock.com (hand)

Storey Publishing
210 MASS MoCA Way
North Adams, MA 01247
storey.com

Printed in China by Shenzhen Reliance Printing Co. Ltd
10 9 8 7 6 5 4 3 2 1

Library of Congress Cataloging-in-Publication Data on file